The Easy Way To Feng Shui

by
Karline McIntosh

PublishAmerica
Baltimore

© 2005 by Karline McIntosh.
All rights reserved. No part of this book may be reproduced, stored in a retrieval system or transmitted in any form or by any means without the prior written permission of the publishers, except by a reviewer who may quote brief passages in a review to be printed in a newspaper, magazine or journal.

First printing

ISBN: 1-4137-5595-X
PUBLISHED BY PUBLISHAMERICA, LLLP
www.publishamerica.com
Baltimore

Printed in the United States of America

This book is dedicated to:

*Michael McIntosh
My husband, who consistently encourages and supports my dreams.*

&

*Jeremie Poulsen
My precious daughter, who inspired this book.*

Special thanks and appreciation to:

*Vernes Samuels, my beautiful mother,
upon whose shoulder I lean so heavily.*

*My sisters, Claire, Leoney and Grace,
for their reassurance and words of hope through
the hills and valleys of life.*

*My funny, lovable brother Webby,
who always helps me to see the lighter side of everything.*

Foreword

"God writes the Gospel not in the Bible alone, but also on trees, in the flowers and clouds and stars."
—Martin Luther

Feng shui is an old philosophy that originated in China. Literally translated, the words *feng* and *shui* mean "wind" and "water."

Initially, I was hesitant to reveal the fact that I was studying and applying the principles of feng shui to my life. Afraid that my friends and family would think that I was tossing my faith in God to the curb or trying to practice some type of voodoo. The truth is, feng shui enhanced my spiritual development rather than distracting me from it. This study evoked a greater awareness of the magnificence of the world around me.

After reading hundreds of testimonies of improved life conditions following the use of feng shui, I was convinced that there must be some inherent good in it. I had to look beyond the superstitious connotations and the cultural affiliations of its birthplace to find out for myself why feng shui worked for so many people. Would it work for me?

Always the adventurer, I was also not about to toss aside a philosophy that had been around for thousands of years without some exploration.

I learned that the immutable laws of nature are at the heart of feng shui. It explains the nourishing and destructive cycles of nature's five primary elements: water, earth, wood, fire and metal. How we unwittingly use them to either help or hinder our lives. Specifically, feng shui provides guidelines and formulas that demonstrate how we can benefit from the movement of energy in our surroundings.

This book does not provide an in-depth study of the science of feng shui. Nor does it promote any particular school. It does, however, acknowledge that the practice of traditional feng shui extends far beyond the oversimplification described herein. The step-by-step suggestions provided at the end of each chapter outline the process I used to apply, track and measure the results of a very personal feng shui experiment.

Contents

Chapter One	The Feng Shui Challenge	11
Chapter Two	Clutter, Clutter Everywhere	17
Chapter Three	Finding the Energy Sectors	23
Chapter Four	The Colors of Your Life	27
Chapter Five	Arranging Furniture	31
Chapter Six	Using Nature's Basic Elements	35
Chapter Seven	Empowering with Enhancements	39
Chapter Eight	Feng Shui Remedies	43
Chapter Nine	Life Transformed	47

Chapter One

The Feng Shui Challenge

"The first law of ecology is that everything is related to everything else."
—Barry Commoner

My 1989 Camry crawled grudgingly up the winding path, crunching pinecones and sending squirrels scampering into trees. After a four-hour drive from Melbourne, I was happy to see the little gray cottage peering at me through clusters of cabbage palms.

No one was home. I could tell by the way the fading lime green curtains hugged the windows.

Good, I thought. *Finally, a chance to kick my feet up and just relax. Maybe watch some television or review my study material on feng shui that I had hurriedly shoved into my overnight bag.*

I turned the car off and stepped onto the graveled driveway. Towering pine trees rustled by the warm Naples breeze tossed their sun-drenched straws like darts in every direction. I brushed the golden needles from my hair as I walked towards the house.

A soft smile raised the corners of my lips as I reached for and felt the key under the empty terra cotta pot at the side of the door.

"Some things never change," I whispered.

I rubbed the key against my jeans to remove the clumps of sand that had settled into its crevices. The door opened easily and slammed shut behind me.

I headed straight for Jeremie's room. The bedroom door squeaked, reluctant to open as I pushed against it with my bag. With added pressure it grudgingly acquiesced to my strength and I could see inside.

Pillows, books, clothes, lots of clothes and papers were fighting for space on the large queen-size bed that blocked the only window in the room. Just inches away from the foot of the bed was an oversized dresser laden with stereo equipment, a thirteen-inch television set, and a three-tiered jewelry box spilling its tangled contents from half-opened miniature drawers. And yes, there was more. Framed photographs, a mascara wand, pens in a range of colors, yellow notepaper and large black and white paper clips utilized every square inch on the top of that dresser.

In a narrow closet, handbags and boxes bulging with more paper climbed toward the ceiling from a metal shelf. Below, more clothes hanging precariously on wire hangers drooped towards piles and piles of shoes.

Clutter, clutter everywhere heralded myriads of feng shui taboos.

At the time of my visit, my twenty-three-year-old daughter Jeremie was a full-time student at Florida Gulf Coast University, majoring in accounting. She also had two part-time jobs and a very active social life.

After living with a couple of roommates and being away at school in Tallahassee for a year, she had accumulated enough stuff to furnish two apartments. Now she was sharing this small two-bedroom cottage with her grandmother. Despite the fact that she used a storage facility, her tiny bedroom could not accommodate all the other things she believed were necessary to her everyday life. Soon after settling in, Jeremie began to experience various problems.

After six years working at the First National Bank of Naples, she was feeling restless and unhappy. Thinking that she needed a change, she considered looking for another position. But shuffling a hectic school schedule, studying, and also waitressing at night, already demanded mental acrobatics just to keep up. And yet, these jobs barely enabled her to make payments on a car that always seemed to be breaking down. And to top it all, she couldn't seem to get her love life on track.

"My life feels like it's spiraling out of control," she often lamented.

There was no doubt about it; Jeremie needed help and lots of it.

So, there it was. Like a veil slowly slipping from my face, everything I had been studying began to make perfect sense to me. Based on the principles of feng shui, the cause of Jeremie's problems was rooted in this room. My heartbeat quickened. Maybe there was something to feng shui after all!

Inhaling deeply, I closed my mouth and cautiously stepped inside the room, trying not to step on a silky red-and-black shirt that seemed to have found respite on the fading peach carpet. I knew what I had to do. But would she agree to a feng shui makeover?

Just then, the phone rang, piercing the silence.

"Hey, Mom, did you just get in?"

"Eh, huh, yes, just walked in," I mumbled.

"I'm gonna be here for another five hours," she said apologetically. "Ade is in Miami."

"Okay," I said absentmindedly. "Jeremie, would you mind very much if I cleaned up your room?"

She hesitated for a moment. Then laughed.

"That would be great, Mom. thanks."

Good, that was all I needed. Permission to proceed! There was no reason to go into elaborate explanations about feng shui experiments and all that. After all, why complicate the matter?

I had been studying about feng shui for nine months when I happened onto Jeremie's chaotic room. At that time, I must say, I was becoming a skeptic because, although I had applied its principles to my living environment, it didn't seem to be impacting my life in any significant way. Or so I thought at the time. Everything I had done up until then had been sporadic attempts based on whatever information was presented to me in any given moment. It was very difficult to tell whether feng shui worked or not without documenting and tracking the results.

Here before me was the perfect opportunity to validate, in a controlled environment, everything I had been learning about feng shui. A small bedroom and a very unhappy occupant with specific problems in important areas of her life literally begged for a feng shui makeover. I'd say this was a feng shui experiment waiting to happen. Results following this experiment, I reasoned, would be measurable.

Feng shui challenges us to live in awareness of our surroundings. It throws a light on the hidden corners of our living spaces and provides specific guidelines to help us benefit from the movement of energy in our environment. The primary focus of this practice is to show human beings how to align themselves with the forces of nature to achieve a more balanced life.

The threads of practical suggestions interwoven into its teaching had been the driving force behind my continued interest in the subject. For personal reasons, I wanted to demystify feng shui's ancient secrets.

"No wonder you are overwhelmed, young lady," I said, flinging my hands in the air.

Since Jeremie had given me permission to clean up the room, I was eager to begin. Because I would be doing a complete makeover, I had to get a big jump on the work before she came home. That would be in approximately five or six hours. There was absolutely no time to waste.

Moving hastily, I exchanged my white shirt and black Capris for a yellow tank top and comfortable brown shorts. Shoes off, and I was ready. Bracing myself for the work ahead, I bent down and picked up the red-and-black shirt from the floor.

And so it began! That hour, that day, that weekend, recorded in snapshot detail, every thought, every word, every action that charted a new course for two lives. A course that would be mapped out by the ancient philosophy of feng shui.

Preparing for Change

* Stand outside your home. Pretend that you are a visitor, seeing your house for the first time.

* Pay special attention to your front door, as this is where energy enters the home. Make a note of anything that creates embarrassment or diminishes your sense of well-being, such as: a leaky pipe, broken light fixtures, unsightly clutter, cracked flowerpots, dead plants or a rusty door handle.

* Go inside and evaluate each space, room by room. Observe the primary colors in the room, and the condition of your furniture. If you have paintings on the walls, what are they depicting? Are the images depressing or uplifting? Observe the shapes of decorative accessories? Be aware of sharp edges and where they are pointing.

* Make a list of everything that you need to change. For example…

* Trim overgrown hedge, replace tattered doormat, clean windows, repaint bedroom, etc.

* Imagine how you would ideally want your home to look and write it down or make a collage from pictures. Work on one space at a time.

* Decide what changes you can make right away, without spending any money, to move you towards the home you have envisioned.

* Find out what it would cost to reach your goal, then act as if there are no obstacles, financial or otherwise, to achieving this dream.

* Create an affirmation in your own words and read it often. For example…

> "My living room is exactly as I want it to be. I spend many hours with my family and friends enjoying the ambiance of this room."

* Spend some time each day quietly visualizing the result you want.

* Empower your desires with emotion. Get excited and give thanks for it even though it has not yet manifested.

Chapter Two

Clutter, Clutter Everywhere

"Let the clean air blow the cobwebs from your body. Air is medicine."
—Lillian Russell

The definition of clutter in the Merriam Webster Dictionary is "to fill or cover with scattered or disordered things that impede movement or reduce effectiveness." Clutter results when there is an overabundance of things. It is a clear indication that we have lost control of our environment. All feng shui practitioners agree that clutter is, simply, bad feng shui.

Getting rid of clutter is probably one of the fastest ways to bring about changes in your environment and increase feelings of well-being. It's a simple concept. Clutter causes confusion. It produces stagnant energy that symbolically blocks your path and hinders personal growth and development.

I began the feng shui process by first evaluating what needed to be done and deciding exactly what I wanted to accomplish. With pen and paper in hand, I stood at the doorway and began to write. My list looked something like this…

a. Need smaller bed.
b. Keep window clear.
c. Organize closet. Make everything accessible.
d. Arrange furniture to maximize floor space.
e. Paint the walls.

f. Choose accent colors.
g. Shampoo the carpet.
h. Sort items in dresser drawers and dump old or broken items.
I. Give to nearest charity.
j. DECLUTTER, DECLUTTER, DECLUTTER (I got a little carried away with that one.)

Next, I tried to visualize the finished project. Finding it difficult, I decided to write an affirmation that would guide my activities and put things into perspective for me. With a clear objective, it would be easier for me to stay on track as I worked. I also hoped that it would sell Jeremie on the feng shui plans I had for the room.
My affirmation…

> *This bedroom will be a bright, comfortable space that is conducive to rest and rejuvenation. Everything about this room should enhance Jeremie's personal development and overall happiness. This space will establish order and balance to bring about positive changes in all areas of her life.*

I have since learned that it is a no-no to feng shui someone's environment without their knowledge. Lucky for me I was unaware of that little caveat. What fun I would have missed, how Jeremie's life would be different—and I probably wouldn't be writing this book. As they say, ignorance is bliss.

It was a tough job getting everything out of the room. I pulled and dragged the heavy queen-size bed. I was huffing and puffing as it threatened to fall on top of my small 110-pound, five-foot frame. But I wasn't going to give in, nor was I about to give up. Finally, the heavy mattress was leaning over the sofa in the living room. The box spring proved to be an easier task. It was much lighter, and I quickly had it propped up against a wall in her grandmother's bedroom.

Approximately three hours after I had begun, everything was out of the room, including the drapes and the closet doors. It had taken me much longer than I had hoped and I was totally exhausted. But I pressed on nonetheless.

Out came the vacuum, dusting rags and Windex. Cobwebs and dirt clung tenaciously to my cleaning cloths. The floor was the worst.

THE EASY WAY TO FENG SHUI

The peach carpet was worn and sun-bleached in spots. I tried cleaning it with a wet vacuum, which did little more than lift the surface dirt. I guess I went a little overboard with the shampooing process, because I now had a damp spot in the middle of the room. I opened the windows, turned the ceiling fan on and left the room to dry out.

Finally, the cleaning frenzy was over. I was surrounded by boxes and mired deep in dust and grime when Jeremie came home. Her eyes narrowed to slits and her mouth opened but no audible sound came out. I knew from her expression that I had better explain, and in as few words as possible, why everything she owned was sitting in piles on the living room floor.

"Feng shui," I said, aware of a feigned begging tone in my voice.

Pretty brown eyes closed and opened again. She dropped her bag and it landed in one of the empty dresser drawers sitting close to the door.

"Mom?" she said, exasperation dripping from every syllable. "What on earth?"

She didn't finish the question. She didn't have to. I didn't respond either. We just stared at each other.

Then, there was a sigh of—understanding, relief or resignation? I wasn't sure which. Either way, I felt safer now. A smile dimpled her cheeks and a look of acquiescence replaced that of horror.

"You said I could clean up, didn't you?"

"Clean up, not destroy," she said, smiling now and flopping down on the only available space on the peach-and-green sofa.

"You're gonna thank me one day," I said with a conviction I didn't feel.

"We'll see, we'll see," she replied, already kicking her shoes off, her eyes fixed on a pile of shoes that I had slated for the dump.

Luckily, we had talked extensively about feng shui in the past nine months. I quickly brought her up to speed with what my plans were for the room. She read the affirmation and despite her initial reticence, I could tell she was getting excited. I got the feeling, however, that she didn't care much whether my feng shui experiment worked or not. Her mess was going away and in its place would be a clean room. That was what mattered to her.

Jeremie's newfound zeal, coupled with my enthusiasm, propelled the decluttering process. After two grueling hours of work, we could hear our stomachs growling. We were both hungry. I kept on working while she made dinner. The smell of fried chicken, mashed potatoes and ripe plantains soon lured me to the table. Leftover broccoli casserole, one of Jeremie's favorite vegetable dishes, topped off the meal.

We lingered after the last bite, sipping wine coolers. That was not a good idea. The wine coolers and all that food made it hard to get back to the task at hand. When we finally began working again, lighthearted banter made the drudgery of our task more bearable. We were still working long after the sun had changed places with the moon. Everything that would go back into the bedroom was carefully organized. Garbage bags brimming with junk were readied for the dump. Boxes stuffed with items for charity or storage were taped up and dragged out to Jeremie's car. Finally, at 2:00 a.m., the decluttering process was done.

It was off to the shower for me. Like standing at the foot of Jamaica's famous Dunns River Falls, the pulsing water whipped my hair into waving wands.

It all felt good. The work that was accomplished, Jeremie's yummy chicken dinner, and now, the soft folds of the bed that caressed my weary body. Lulled by the repetitive whirl of the overhead fan, sleep came quickly.

Clutter

Sort It   Store It   Give It Away   Dump It

* Identify a temporary storage area for the items that you will remove from the selected areas.

* Hang a wind chime or play some upbeat music in this area and be sure to keep it as clean as possible until the decluttering process is over.

* Date and label four boxes: Store, Donate, Garbage, and Sort.

* The Sort Box will hold items that needs to be organized into containers or belong to other areas of the home.

* To find out which container to place all other items, ask yourself:
Do I love it? Do I need it? Does it enhance my life in any way?
Is it worth the time and effort to maintain it?
If you answered no to all these questions, it should be finding its way into one of the following containers.
Storage... of no use to you, but you are not ready to part with it.
Charity... someone else can use it.
Dump... old, broken or dated.

The size of your home and the level of disorganization should determine your decluttering schedule. It is best to work in small increments in order to give your full attention to each space.

Chapter Three

Finding the Energy Centers

"It is in a man's heart that the life of nature's spectacle exists; to see it, one must feel it."
—Jean-Jacques Rousseau

According to feng shui, there are eight major categories that represent the building blocks of our lives. We achieve balance when we recognize their significance to our feelings of well-being and consciously seek ways to cultivate them. Identifying and enhancing these critical areas may determine whether favorable or foul winds blow your way.

Feng shui tells us that the energies that govern these sectors are represented in specific areas in our living environment and suggest various tools to help us to locate them. A very simple method of locating these important energy sectors involves using a fairly popular feng shui tool known as the Bagua Energy Map. This map charts the location of these important life sectors, which are:

Romantic Love—Most people tend to feel lonely, dissatisfied and incomplete without it.

Children—The desire to see our children develop and grow into healthy, happy human beings. It is also important to nurture the child within by making time for play and recreation.

Helpful People—Looking beyond ourselves and recognizing our need for friends, mentors and benefactors. Developing our spiritual life and our faith so that we can weather the storms of life when they inevitably come knocking at our door.

Career—Our daily occupation, whether we work outside of the home or grow peas in a garden. Whatever occupies our days and rewards us through monetary or emotional compensation or both.

Knowledge—Our ongoing quest for knowledge or education for personal growth and development. Growing in wisdom through deep meditation and study.

Family—All our family relationships. Yes, including the relationship with your mother-in-law or that eccentric aunt that drives you nuts.

Wealth—Whatever wealth represents to you. Having a hefty bank account, or non-material riches such as health, good relationships, comfortable home, and healthy, happy children. Great wealth can also be as simple as an ever-deepening feeling of contentment and peace.

Fame—Recognition within your community, among your co-workers or church members. Achieving public acclaim.

Because of the dimensions of the space, it would be very easy to locate the energy sectors in Jeremie's bedroom. Reaching into my handbag, I retrieved the miniature version of the Bagua Energy Map that I had been carrying around for nine months. Just in case!

Sitting at the small dining table in the kitchen, I drew a rough sketch of the bedroom, making sure to pencil in the location of the window, closet and an angled wall at the doorway that extend into the room. I then overlaid the map on the sketch aligning the bottom of the map with the knowledge, career and helpful people sectors along the wall containing the doorway. Next, I scribbled the name of the energy sectors on the sketch of the room. This information would be helpful later when arranging and decorating the space. That was the easy part. Now I had to get ready to paint.

Locating the Energy Centers

* Use the Bagua Map to locate the nine energy centers in your home and individual rooms by positioning the map over the floor plan of your home. Align the bottom of the map with knowledge, career and helpful people along the wall of your home that contains the front door. If applied correctly, the main entrance to your home will fall in one of three areas; knowledge, career or helpful people.

* For two-story homes, a bathroom on the lower level with a bedroom above it would both fall into the same sector. Once you have clearly identified the life areas of your home, apply the same principle to individual rooms.

* Make a note of each energy center on the sketch of your floor plan. Pay special attention to the area of your life that you want to work on first.

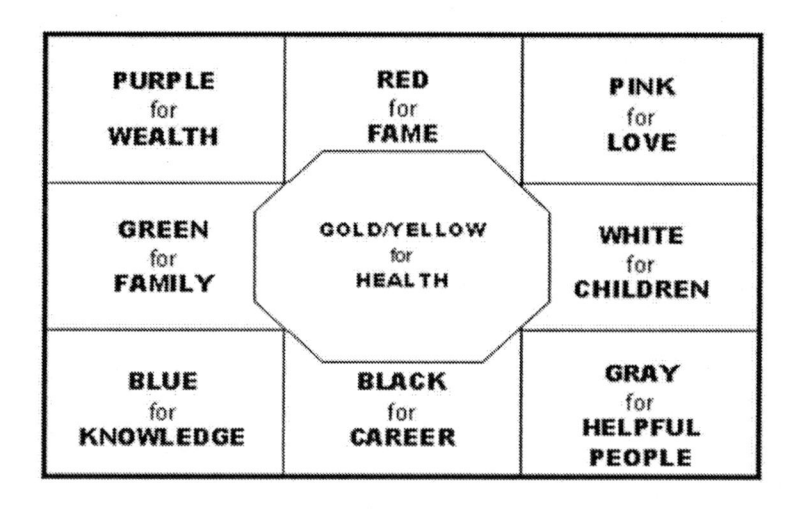

PURPLE for **WEALTH**	**RED** for **FAME**	**PINK** for **LOVE**
GREEN for **FAMILY**	**GOLD/YELLOW** for **HEALTH**	**WHITE** for **CHILDREN**
BLUE for **KNOWLEDGE**	**BLACK** for **CAREER**	**GRAY** for **HELPFUL PEOPLE**

LOCATING THE ENERGY SECTORS
Ideal Floor Plan With No Missing Sectors

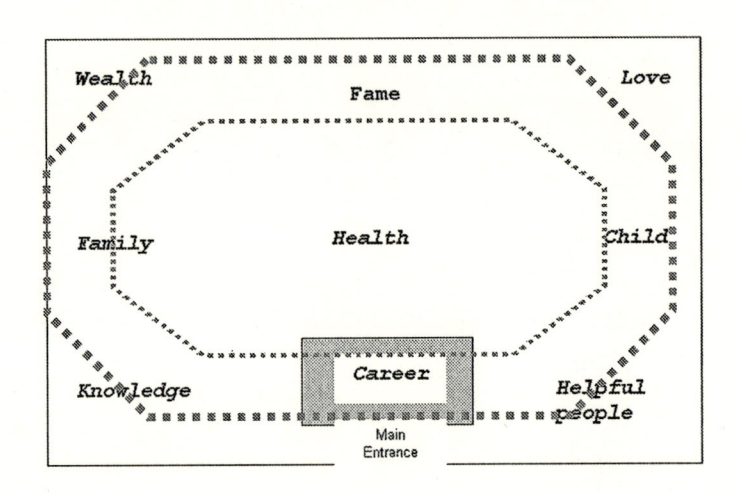

Wealth — *Fame* — *Love*
Family — *Health* — *Child*
Knowledge — *Career* — *Helpful people*

Main Entrance

HOMES WITH MISSING SECTORS

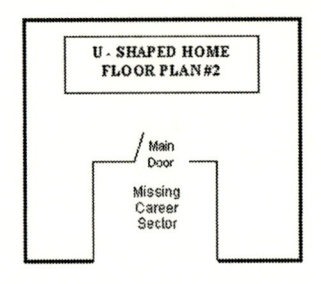

U - SHAPED HOME FLOOR PLAN #2

Main Door
Missing Career Sector

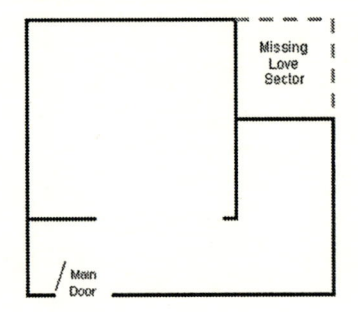

Missing Love Sector

Main Door

Chapter Four

The Colors of Your Life

> "All nature wears one universal grin."
> —Henry Fielding

Let's face it, nature sweeps color across the landscape of our lives and we cannot escape it. The most vibrant color of all runs through our veins. Is it any wonder then that color is such an essential element in feng shui?

Another important aspect of color is its ability to heal, rebalance and refresh. From the ancient Egyptians to modern medicine, color therapy has been used as a method for treating various illnesses. Likewise, color is used in feng shui to activate the flow of energy in specific areas of our homes.

However, the use of bright colors often presents a daunting challenge for some people. It seems easier for the color-shy individual to play it safe and stick with the blank-canvas effect rather than risk making a bad color choice. As a result, the standard color for interior walls is usually white or a derivative of white. Not to worry, feng shui provides a simple answer to this dilemma.

Feng shui recommends specific colors for each life sector that are believed to be beneficial to the designated area. These may be used as primary or accent colors.

Now that the clearing and decluttering process in Jeremie's bedroom was done, the next step was to decide on the color scheme.

I decided that what Jeremie needed most was to feel loved and loving. I selected a soft shade of pink. Before you start to gag, let me explain. In feng shui, pink is a powerful color for attracting love.

The walls warmed up to this pale, almost translucent pink. This soft pink resonated with romance and would cast its spell on everything in the room, including Jeremie and anyone else who visited her there.

Next, I needed a central focus for the room. Sunlight filtering in from the sole window made it the ideal focal point. Dressed in sheer unlined white curtains then layered with wine red cotton drapes, the window treatment created a serene cocoon effect at night. Stylish metal and crystal tiebacks affixed on either side provided a respite for the dark drapes in the daytime. I had no doubt Jeremie would appreciate the duplicity of this design.

On the bed, four large pillows covered in satiny floral fabric snuggled up to a textured tan comforter. The bed ruffle's tan background, splattered with the same floral motif, echoed the primary colors in the drape and comforter. Three black cushions nestled among the pillows introduced just a hint of formality to this casual space.

Color is probably the first thing you notice when you enter a room. It can make a room seem large or small, bright and cheery, or dark and depressing. Feng shui recommends specific colors for each life sector. These colors, however, have universal appeal.

Purple is recommended to enhance the wealth sector. A powerful color, purple has long been associated with royalty. It evokes a sense of majesty and in ancient times was mostly worn by the very rich or high-ranking clergies of the church.

However, it helps to be "color savvy" when using purple, as too much can create a gothic effect. Unless, of course, that's the effect you are aiming for. Teamed with other colors, purple can greatly enrich stark spaces.

Red is powerful and dramatic. It is easy to understand why this vibrant color is recommended for the fame sector. The power of red brings the fire element and its accompanying energy force to dominate wherever it is used. By all means use it, but keep it under control or it may stir up fire-related accidents in the home. Don't, however; overlook the power of this magnificent color if you want to get noticed. Keep it in the fame sectors of the home, where it will be most effective.

Pink fuels romance and is said to cast a radiant glow to one's complexion. Use one of its softer shades in conjunction with other colors in the bedroom and especially in the love corner. Try to overlook the negative connotations that sometimes surround this color. It bodes very well indeed for those seeking happiness in love.

Green is one of the dominant colors found in nature and is recommended by feng shui to be used to strengthen and support the family sector. It represents growth, promotes healing and belief in one's own potential. The varying shades and its close affiliation with yellow, make it a popular choice in most living environments.

Yellow is a warm, friendly color that represents stability and strength. It is recommended for use in the health sector, at the center of the home or property. Use this color to bring laughter and happiness into your life, but do not overpower the space with it. Team yellow with orange to fill the room with vibrant energy.

White represents purity and is the color for the children sector. However, an area saturated with this color will ultimately have low levels of energy that can become stagnant. White makes a great backdrop for bright colors. It works best combined with yellow to uplift and energize.

Blue enhances the knowledge sector. Serene and calming, this color aids meditation and study. The mysterious quality and subtleties of blue also beckon you to seek new adventures and explore unfamiliar terrains.

Black works well in the career area symbolizing the formality often associated with the work environment. Black also represents water due to its mysterious qualities. Use black's cool introspective nature to bring drama to your home, but quench its overpowering presence with softer, warmer hues.

Gray hovers like a guardian angel between black and white. Associated with spirituality and travel, use this color to enhance the helpful people sector. It makes a superb backdrop for more brilliant shades such as red, orange or yellow. It also works extremely well with blue—however, be careful with this mix, as these are both cool colors and can create too much of a cold environment.

Simple Cleansing and Reenergizing Ritual

(Use especially after painting a room)

Cleansing

* Clear the space of clutter and dirt before performing this ritual.
* Place a bowl of clean water in the center of the room and let stand for a few hours to absorb negative energy or paint fumes.
* Discard water.

Energizing

* Light nine tea candles and place each one in each of the eight energy sectors. Be sure to place them in a small dish or candleholder to prevent wax spill or fire. (Do not leave candles unattended).
* Burn a stick of incense in the center of the room. Allow the candles and incense to burn out naturally. Once they are extinguished, remove them from the room.
* Energize the space with music of your choice. The tinkling sound of wind chimes, bells or clapping hands also helps to stimulate the flow of energy in the space.

Chapter Five

Arranging Furniture

"The truly healthy environment is not merely safe, but stimulating."
—William H. Stewart

Creating comfortable indoor living environments that allow energy to circulate freely is what feng shui calls "balancing chi." Achieving balance may be as simple as re-arranging your furniture to create a cozier living environment. Harmonious living is achieved when balance reigns and life feels more like a beautiful adventure than a daily grind.

Creating an energy-friendly environment in Jeremie's tiny bedroom proved to be somewhat of a challenge. Apart from the dimensions of the space, it had irregular angles projecting into the room.

Originally, the scale of the furniture overwhelmed the small space. The large dresser and bed dominated the room and were receptacles for everything that had no designated place. But the bed was the worst, as it covered most of the floor, inhibiting movement. There was just no way around it. The bed had to go.

Trading in the queen-size bed for a small day bed was my only option. I placed the bed diagonal to the doorway so that Jeremie would be able to easily see anyone approaching her room. With the bed tucked into the corner, it was also no longer visible in the mirror. This complied with an important feng shui stipulation that a bed should never be reflected in a mirror. Don't you just love the way feng shui pays attention to practical details to reduce stress in our lives?

Coated with a mix of wall paint and polyurethane, the large dresser and wood-surround mirror was returned to its original position in the room. Its new façade, however, merged artfully with the wall color to diminish its presence. The mirror reflecting the window infused the room with light. The illusion of a second window created by the mirror not only balanced the space but also produced a dynamic connection to the outside world.

The only new addition to the room was a white wicker table rescued from the back porch. Topped with clear glass it effected a seamless segue to everything placed beneath it. Placing the stereo equipment under this table proved very doable now that clutter was no longer a problem.

Too much electrical equipment in the bedroom defied an important feng shui rule. Space issues, however, made it impossible to comply and would therefore require a feng shui remedy.

That was it, a bed, dresser and the glass table. Three major pieces of furniture was all this tiny space could accommodate. Oh, I almost forgot. A tall wooden CD holder was placed in the corner next to the door.

And we must not forget the closet. The ruthless elimination of anything that was no longer relevant to Jeremie's current lifestyle increased the functionality of this space. The addition of shoe racks, new hangers, and clear containers restored order and balance. Everything was now visible and accessible. Replacing the freshly painted doors brought closure to the closet renovation.

Movement without entanglement was now possible. Jeremie had to at least be grateful for that.

Bedrooms are designed for rest and rejuvenation. However, in our hectic modern lives, this most sacred space often becomes a repository for everything from televisions, food trays, to desks, computers and stereo equipment. When decorating the bedroom, keep its primary function in mind and think about what all that electrical equipment is doing to you while you are sleeping.

Arranging Your Furniture

Answer the following questions before you start rearranging your furniture:

1. What is the primary function of that space?
2. What type of activities will be performed there?
3. How many people will have access to the room?
4. How do you want the room to look and feel?

* Arrange living room furniture to form an octagon, rectangle or square. Avoid L- or U-shaped arrangements.

* Place sofas so that they have some form of support behind them, such as a wall, table or plants.

* Place frequently used couches, beds and desks so that occupants can get a clear view of anyone entering the room.

* Arrange your bed so that it is not reflected in any mirrors in the bedroom.

* Spend some time in each room after rearranging the furniture to heighten your awareness of how the space feels.

Chapter Six

Using Nature's Basic Elements

"Nature never did betray the heart that loved her."
—William Wordsworth

The study of feng shui encompasses the belief that human beings are fundamentally connected to five elements of nature... wood, fire, earth, metal and water. These elements describe the essential qualities of energy and operate on two very distinct cycles, the nourishing and destructive cycles. Harnessing the predictive power of these elements, however, involves understanding their complementary yet opposite cycles.

In the nourishing cycle: water feeds wood, wood fuels fire, fire replenishes the earth, the earth produces metal and metal is a receptacle for water. By contrast, in the destructive cycle: metal cuts wood, wood depletes the earth, earth absorbs water, water extinguishes fire and fire warps metal.

The constant interplay of these elements prevents the predominance of either cycle in order to achieve a state of harmony and balance. As a result, there is always the potential for change from hot to cold, chaos to tranquility, sickness to health or poverty to prosperity.

The elements are also linked to specific colors and sectors of the Bagua as shown below:

Element	Color	Sector
Fire	Red	Fame
Metal	White	Children
Water	Black	Career
Wood	Green	Family
Earth	Yellow	Health

Use the elements that nourish each other when you want to activate the areas that they govern. Elements that destroy or transform each other should only be teamed to restore balance when there is an overabundance of any one element in a space.

Activate fire energy in the fame area when you are seeking upward movement and recognition. Stabilize your life with the earth element by incorporating the grounding colors of yellow or brown in the health area at the center of the home. Metal strengthens your resolve and helps you to stay focused. The water element helps to generate movement when things get stuck.

Understanding the five elements and how they interact will clue you into which element to use where and why you are using it.

Working with the five elements in Jeremie's bedroom was a lot easier than I had expected. The first step was to evaluate the room to see whether these elements were already situated in their proper locations.

Beginning with the fame sector, I immediately noticed the presence of the fire element in the deep red of the drapes at the window. Since I wanted to enhance the love and romance area of Jeremie's life, the passion of the fire element was essential to success.

On the left wall, directly over the bed, a painting of oak trees against a deep green landscape represented the wood element in the family sector. In the closet, white metal shelving provided a subtle representation of metal for the children sector. A black glass vase half filled with water arranged proudly in the career area satisfied the water element.

Okay, that's fire, wood, metal and water. Just one left. Earth.

"What can I use to represent earth," I mumbled.

To answer that question, I headed to a closet filled with rugs, rags and towels.

"Nothing, Nothing, Nothing!"

Exasperated, I was just about to close the door when something yellow peeked at me from behind neatly folded towels and pillowcases.

"Aha!" I shouted excitedly.

I pulled out a yellow throw. It was a little faded, but I shrugged and sauntered back to the bedroom. Once in the room, however, my enthusiasm evaporated like beads of water on a hot stove. It just looked out of place and surely did not complement the existing color palate of the room.

Feng Shui is like that sometimes. It doesn't always work with your décor. That's when you have to decide what is more important. If you are to accomplish your feng shui goals, you may need to sacrifice form for function.

Jeremie would never go for it, so I decided to make an executive decision. I returned the throw to the closet and moved on.

THE FIVE ELEMENTS

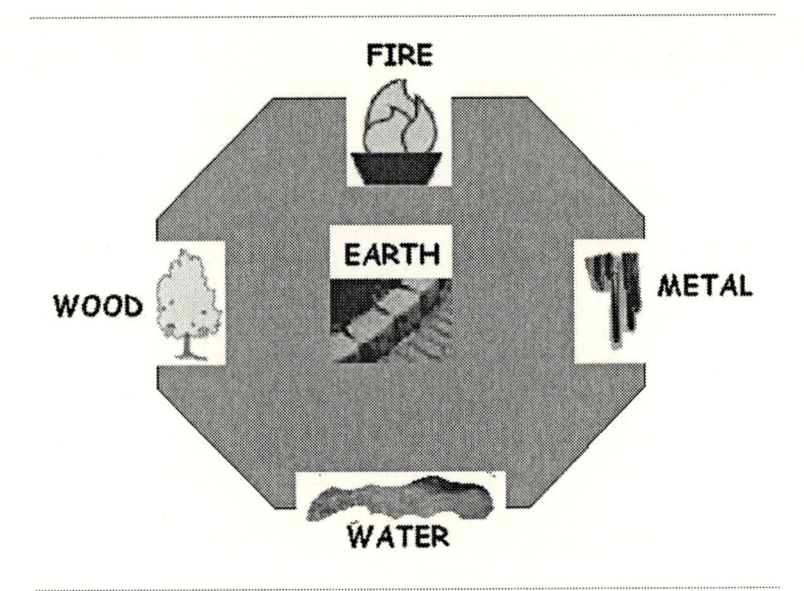

Chapter Seven

Empowering with Enhancements

"He who knows what sweets and virtues are in the ground, the waters, the plants, the heavens, and how to come at these enchantments, is the rich and royal man."
—Ralph Waldo Emerson

The next morning, I woke up to a quiet house. Jeremie had already left for work. I was on my own. The first hour of the day was spent choosing enhancements for her room. The choices had to reflect the results that I was trying to achieve, as well as complement the existing decor.

Although I know better now, at that time, I was not aware of the admonition to enhance gradually. Boosting the energies in too many areas at once may result in a period of confusion caused by shifting energy patterns.

Ah well, ignorance reigned as I set about to enhance every life sector of that bedroom.

Traditional feng shui utilizes a host of objects to energize each life category. These are called enhancements. They help to activate energy shifts that bring about change when used in the life sectors. I have found that enhancements are most powerful when empowered with purpose and meaning to the individual using them.

To begin, I hung a small multi-faceted crystal in the window. Crystals are said to be imbued with vibrant energy and are intensified by light. I imagined a kaleidoscope of color dancing around the room when the bright morning sun collided with the crystal. An added incentive to this enhancement was that the mirror facing the window would duplicate this splendor.

There was only one place for Jeremie's television. You guessed it, on the large dresser, exactly where it was before. The only difference now was that the stereo was no longer sitting next to it. However, this worked for the knowledge sector, because televisions and computers are recent additions to feng shui enhancements.

Enhancement number three was already in place in the black vase enhancing the career sector.

The door into the room was located in the helpful people sector. The CD holder placed there earlier represented people bringing music into Jeremie's life. And, to further enhance the area, I hung several photos of Jeremie and her friends laughing and having fun on the beach, at each others' homes and at parties.

Corny as all that sounds, I was very proud of myself for that one.

The children sector was impossible to personalize. So I decided to leave that to chance. You just can't win them all. Of course, in this case it was truly a blessing. I had long since met my enhancement quota.

Hold on, I'm not finished. For the marriage sector, I pulled out the heavy weights. My feng shui notes. I had to get this one right. This was the love area, which everyone would agree is of vital importance to a happy life.

Feng Shui recommend using items in two's. I selected a photo portraying a young couple whose wedding Jeremie had recently attended. The photo of the smiling couple was already in a heart-shaped frame, which was ideal for this area. Two red candles, which I would constantly remind her to light, should do the job.

Enhancement Suggestions

Career: Use a water fountain or bird feeder in the front yard to increase the flow of energy and career opportunities. A melodious wind chime is a classic enhancement for this space.

Love/Marriage: Decorate this space with universal symbols of love in pairs. Mandarin ducks, doves or dolphins suggest a lasting relationship. Light a couple of candles regularly to ignite love's passion. Roses and peonies also attract romance.

Wealth & Prosperity: Place items that imply the flow of wealth, such as three vases in varying sizes filled with coins. A popular wealth symbol is the three-legged frog with a coin in his mouth. Place it on a low table or under a chair across from the main entrance into your home. Grow plants that bloom purple flowers in the wealth section of your property.

Fame: Enhance this area when seeking recognition and public acclaim. Use the color red or any fire element, such as a working fireplace or candles. This is also the ideal place for written affirmations or objects that represent your goals or past career achievements such as letters of commendation, diplomas, certificates and trophies.

Family: If you have ever struggled with finding the best place for your exercise equipment, this is it. Decorate this area with healthy plants, clear crystals and rectangular objects. Hang beautifully framed family photos in this sector.

Children: This is where you can lighten up and have some fun. Treat this area with splashes of color, against a white background. This is the place for whimsical artwork, children's photos and musical instruments. This is also the ideal place for a baby's room. If you are trying to conceive, place a fertility symbol in this sector. The pomegranate represents fertility because of its many seeds.

Helpful People: Energize the front right section of the Bagua Map to attract more helpful people and travel opportunities. This area governs people who can help you in life, such as spiritual guides, mentors, saints and friends. Bring out your religious icons and set up your home altars here. If there are people in your life who can mentor or inspire you to achieve your goals, place their picture, a book they have written or their business card in this quadrant.

Knowledge: This sector governs personal growth and development. Use a bright light, paintings of mountains or ships sailing toward you. Electrical equipment such as a televisions or computers are recognized for their power to activate energy.
Remember to use enhancements that have meaning and purpose to you. Keep them simple and apply gradually. They should reflect the results you are seeking as well as enhance the aesthetics of the space.

Chapter Eight

Feng Shui Remedies

"Nature provides exceptions to every rule."
—Margaret Fuller

One of the main teachings of feng shui is that the condition of your surroundings can have a direct impact on your health and overall well being.

Energy is an integral component of life, and how it circulates around us is important. According to feng shui, *shar chi*, otherwise known as "negative energy," causes all forms of misfortune and disaster. But before we can cure negative energy patterns, we must first identify the cause. One way to open your "feng shui eyes" is to become more aware of your surroundings.

Energy flows easily and peacefully around us when it is allowed to meander. Fast-moving energy, traveling along straight lines, can be injurious to human beings. Long narrow corridors and hallways are infamous for generating harmful energy. Remember that the primary purpose of applying a cure is to prevent stagnant, piercing or rushing energy in our living spaces.

Various time-proven elements have been endorsed by feng shui masters to stabilize negative vibrations. For instance, screens, curtains and room dividers are cures that block out bad views and so-called poison arrows. Lights dissolve, sounds dispel, screens block, mirrors deflect, and so on.

I was finally at the remedial stage of this bedroom transformation. Correcting negative feng shui situations such as the overabundance of electrical equipment in the small space or any sharp angles was at the top of my list. The projection where the walls of the closet met also represented a poison arrow shooting at Jeremie every time she entered the room.

To remedy the electromagnetic field problem, a small plant in a terra cotta pot was arranged on the floor beside the stereo. Next to the television, a silky green plant helped to defuse the negative energies there. For the sharp, pointy wall, decorative curly ribbons suspended from the ceiling mimicked a cascading waterfall.

If there were any additional problems, they were not readily apparent to me. Because I had started with an empty space, it was easy to create an environment that was basically free of bad feng shui.

The key to a safe, comfortable home is to be aware of and remove any hostile or aggressive images, objects or pieces of furniture with sharp or pointy edges that may cause physical injury. The fluid nature of energy requires unobstructed paths through which to flow. If the design element of any room in your home feels unsafe for children, you can be sure negative energy patterns exist there.

Being cognizant of your surroundings, both inside and out, will draw your attention to the problem areas. Keep your cures simple and make a note of the date and type of cure used in order to track results.

A feng shui cure is like a balm that soothes and heals a wound. And just like a balm, you must give it time to work.

Feng Shui Remedies

It is not always possible to create the perfect feng shui environment. As a result, feng shui offers solutions otherwise known as "cures" or "remedies" that alleviate or improve these negative situations.

Some negative feng shui situations include:

* Working at a desk with your back to the door.
* A bedroom with multiple mirrors causing the bed to be reflected in a mirror.
* A cluttered living or working environment.
* Sharp edges that can cause injury.
* A leaky toilet.
* A bathroom situated in the center of the home.
* Overgrown hedges that block the path to your door.
* Straight paths such as long corridors or driveways.
* Stairs that lead directly out of your front door.
* Bedrooms situated directly under a bathroom.
* Cooking with your back to the door
* Negative placement of the five elements, etc.

Remedies operate on two distinct levels: mundane and transcendental.

Mundane remedies include rearranging your furniture, using mirrors to expand a space, crystals to activate and disperse energy, wind chimes to moderate the flow of energy, plants to nourish and cleanse, moving water such as aquariums and fountains to energize, and light to dispel, lift and circulate energy. Symbolic representations of the five elements are the best remedial tools for negative energy patterns.

Transcendental remedies include focused energy in the form of meditation, affirmations, prayer and rituals that help us to reinforce our intentions.

Chapter Nine

Life Transformed

"Life is a daring adventure or nothing."
—Helen Keller

Exhausted but satisfied with the bedroom makeover, I returned to Melbourne. If nothing else, I told myself, Jeremie now had a clean, organized bedroom in which to live. For me, the feng shui experiment would only be considered a success if radical changes followed and in quick succession.

It wasn't long before the changes began. The first few days after the transformation, Jeremie told me that she felt so much better in her new environment. She stopped complaining about headaches. No surprise there. The room was beautiful and very organized.

Three months after the makeover, at the end of the fall semester, Jeremie decided to take a year off from her studies at Gulf Coast University. I was not happy with that decision. I wanted her to progress, not regress. Feng shui does caution, however, that as energy shifts occur, changes may appear disruptive at first. I decided to allow the process to evolve without judgment.

In January, just months later, she was offered and accepted a full-time position at the bank. With her new job, Jeremie's finances began to improve immediately and she was soon able to give up her part-time waitressing position. Although I was unhappy that she had put school on the back burner, I had to admit, things were happening.

Following the transformation of her bedroom, she began inviting friends over to the cottage. It was during this time that some new "helpful people" came into her life. Their presence and influence helped her to grow spiritually. This new development led to a very important decision that she had been contemplating for a long time. Jeremie donned a white dress and was immersed in water baptism.

In July, her grandmother sold the cottage, which forced Jeremie to seek a new home. She moved into an apartment that was approximately fifteen minutes from her workplace.

In August, exactly one year after the makeover, Jeremie received a proposal for marriage. She accepted, and the flurry of activities surrounding the planning of a wedding began.

Six months later, Jeremie exchanged vows at the Palm Bay Methodist Church in Palm Bay, Florida. After a seven-day honeymoon cruise, she returned to a new life, a new home and a new name.

Closing Notes

"I hear and I forget, I see and I remember, I do and I understand."
—Confucius

Feng Shui was discovered in China thousands of years ago. Over the years, it has evolved and adapted to various cultures and lifestyles. This evolution has spawned various schools and methodologies that are the source of confusion for most people just learning about it. Because feng shui also comes to us layered with the cultural norms and traditions of China, its practical teaching is often overlooked.

The important thing to remember is that at the heart of feng shui is the premise that human beings can improve the quality of their lives by balancing the flow of energy in their surroundings. Feng shui provides specific guidelines to accomplish this seemingly formidable task.

There is truly no mystery behind the suggestion to not sleep under a drafty window or to bring the elements of nature into your living space to create a more tranquil environment. Neither is it surprising that you will benefit by designing your bedroom to be soothing and conducive to rest and rejuvenation.

Although it takes many years of study and practical application to be recognized as a feng shui master, you don't have to master feng shui to enjoy the benefits of this practical science. The gift feng shui will bring to your life is a greater awareness of your interconnection with everything around you. It may lead you to appreciate the resplendence of color and to recognize that nature's destructive and nourishing cycles are natural and essential. You may even become more in sync with the ebb and flow of your own life experience. No longer will you take for granted the laws of the universe that has been so ordered to benefit all.

Once you learn the basic principles and specific guidelines, it is easy to understand what changes need to be made and why. When your living and working environments are balanced and orderly, your stress levels are diminished and your health, wealth and happiness potential increase tremendously.

The goal in acquiring knowledge about feng shui and applying its principles is to maximize the good things in your life and remove obstacles imposed by negative influences in your environment.

The most fascinating truth I have learned about feng shui is that it works, whether we believe it or not!